Arduino Programming for Beginners in Projects and Examples

How to Get Started

Table of Contents

Introduction

Arduino is a nice programming language, especially when it comes to hardware programming. It comes as a prototype, made up of both the hardware and the software parts. The hardware part is what is programmed, and the programming is done from the software part, which is usually the IDE (Integrated Development Environment). Most robots in use currently have been developed with Arduino as the programming language. This is because one can use Arduino to instruct the robot do something under a wide variety of circumstances. The language is also easy for anyone to understand. This book makes this much simple. Enjoy reading!

Chapter 1- What is Arduino?

Arduino is an open source prototype platform with hardware and software which is easy to use. It has a circuit board which we can program, and software referred to as Arduino IDE which we can use for writing and uploading the computer code to our physical board.

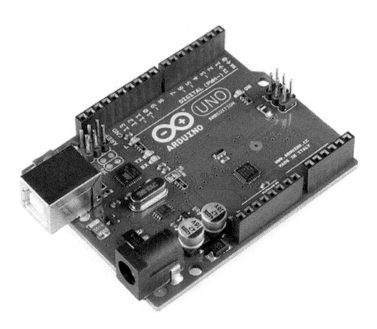

The Arduino boards are capable of reading both analog and digital signals from the different sensors, and then turning this into an output like turning a LED on/off, activating a motor, or establishing a connection to the cloud. The board functions can be controlled by sending some set of instructions to our microcontroller located on the board through the Arduino IDE.

Chapter 2- Installation

We need to set up the Arduino IDE. It is after this that we will be in a position to upload our code to the Arduino board. This is a very important part in Arduino programming, as you can do nothing if don't have the environment set ready for programming.

You should have the Arduino board with you and a USB cable. If you use Arduino UNO, Nano, Arduino Duemilanove, Diecimila, or Arduino Mega 2560, then ensure that you have a standard USB cable with you.

If you are using Arduino Nano, you should have the A to Mini-B cable.

Download the Arduino IDE. Visit the official website for Arduino to download the correct version of the Arduino IDE. Once the download is complete, unzip the file.

You can then power up the board. Arduino Uno, Duemilanove, Mega, and Arduino Nano are capable of drawing power from an external power supply or from a USB connected to a computer. For users of Arduino Diecimila, ensure that your board has been configured so as to draw power from a USB connection. A jumper is used for selecting the power source.

Use a USB cable to connect your Arduino board to the computer.

After that, just launch the Arduino IDE. My assumption is that you unzipped it after the download. Find the application icon from the unzipped folder, and then double-click on it. This will start the IDE.

Now that you have opened the IDE, you can choose to create a new project or launch an already existing project.

Click on "New->File" so as to create a new project.

If you need to open an already existing project, just click on "File → Example → Basics → Blink." In this case, we will have opened a project with the name "Blink," and this will cause the LED to blink on and then off with a delay. You can also choose to select any other example from the list.

Errors usually occur whenever we are trying to upload a program to the board. To prevent this from occurring, one has to select the correct name for the Arduino board. This has to match the board which has been connected to your computer.

Just navigate to Tools → Board, and then choose the correct board. At this point, you can choose the serial device of your Arduino board. In most cases, it should be COM3 or a higher one. If you need to find out the port, just disconnect the Arduino board and then open the menu. You will see one of the entries disappear, and this should be the one for the Arduino board. You can then reconnect it, and then choose that serial port.

Now, you can upload your program to the board. The Arduino IDE toolbar has some symbols. Click on the one for Upload (->). Wait for few seconds, and you will observe both TX and RX LEDS on your board begin to flash. If the process of uploading runs successfully, then you will see the message "Done uploading" displayed on the status bar.

Chapter 3- Structure of Arduino Programs

In Arduino, the programs are usually made up of three parts:

1. Structure

2. Values

3. Functions

The structure part is made up of two main functions:

- Setup( ) function

- Loop( ) function

The "setup()" function is usually called once we have started a sketch. We use the pin modes for the purpose of initialization of variables, and for allowing us to begin using libraries.

Void setup ( ) {

}

The loop() function is used when we want to loop consecutively. This will give our program some room for making changes and responding appropriately.

Chapter 4- Variables and Constants

Variables and constants are of great importance in a programming language. The difference between the two is that after declaration of a variable, one can change its value, but once a constant has been declared, its value cannot be changed. For instance, if you try to change the value of a constant, you will get an error. The two are used for reserving some space in the computer memory for a particular value. Arduino supports the use of variables in programming, and these variables have a scope. Scope refers to a region in the program. It specifies the place in which we can declare a variable.

- Local variables can be declared inside a block or a function

- Formal parameters refers to the definition of the parameters of a function

- Global variables are defined outside all other functions

Local Variables

These are the variables defined inside a block or function. These can only be accessed by the statements which have been defined inside that block or function. If you try to access a local outside its function of declaration, then you will get an error as the variable will not be found. Consider the example given below:

```
Void setup () {
}
Void loop () {
  int a , b ;
  int c ; Local variable declaration
  a = 0;
  b = 0; actual initialization
  c = 5;
}
```

Global Variables

These are the variables defined outside the functions and most probably and the top. Use them to hold a value throughout the life of your program. You can use any function to access a global variable, despite its location within the program. Consider the following example:

```
Int T , S ;
float z = 0 ; Global variable declaration
Void setup () {
}

Void loop () {
   int a , b ;
   int c ; Local variable declaration
   a = 0;
   b = 0; actual initialization
   c = 5;
}
```

Chapter 5- Operators

These are symbols which instruct the compiler to carry out a specific mathematical or logical operation. Let us discuss some of the operators supported in Arduino.

Arithmetic Operators

These include the assignment operator (=), addition (+), subtraction (-), multiplication (*), division (/), and modulo (%).

Consider the following example:

```
void loop () {
   int x = 5, y = 3,c;
   z= x + y;
   z = x - y;
   z = x * y;
   z = x / y;
   z = x % y;
}
```

The above example should give you the following as the output:

x + y = 8
x - y = 2
x * y = 15
x / y = 2

Comparison Operators

These are used for comparison purposes. They include equal to (==), not equal to (!=), less than (<), greater than (>), less than or equal to (<=), greater than or equal to (>=). Consider the following example:

void loop () {

```
    int x = 5,y = 3
    bool z = false;
    if(x == y)
      z = true;
    else
      z = false;

    if(x != y)
      z = true;
    else
      z = false;

    if(x < y)
      z = true;
    else
      z = false;

    if(x > y)
      z = true;
    else
      z = false;

    if(x <= y)
      z = true;
    else
      z = false;

    if(x >= y)
      z = true;
    else
      z = false;
}
```

Execution of the program should give you the following result:

z = false
z = true
z = false
z = true

z = false
z = false

Boolean Operators

These include and (&&), or (||), and not (!). The following example demonstrates how these can be used:

```
void loop () {
  int x = 5,y = 3
  bool z = false;
  if((x > y)&& (y < x))
    z = true;
  else
    z = false;

  if((x == y)|| (y < x))
    z = true;
  else
    z = false;

  if( !(x == y)&& (y < x))
    z = true;
  else
    z = false;
}
```

The above program should give you the following output after execution:

```
z = true
z = true
z = true
```

Bitwise Operators

These include and (&), or (|), xor (^), not (~), shit left (<<), and shift right (>>). Consider the following example:

```
void loop () {
  int x = 5, y = 10
  int z = 0;
```

```
    z = x & y ;
    z = x | y ;
    z = x ^ y ;
    z = x ~ y ;
    z = x << y ;
    z = x >> y ;
}
```

Their operation on the numbers is done in a binary format.

Compound Operators

These include the increment (++), decrement (--), compound addition (+=), compound subtraction (-=), compound multiplication (*=), compound division (/=), compound modulo (%=), compound bitwise or (|=), and compound bitwise and (&=).

Consider the following example:

```
void loop () {
    int x = 5,y = 10
    int z = 0;

    x++;
    x--;
    y += x;
    y -= x;
    y *= x;
    y /= x;
    x %= y;
    x |= y;
    x &= y;
}
```

Chapter 6- Control Statements

In decision making, the programmer is expected to create a condition which will be evaluated before some statements can be executed. Let us explore some of the control statements in Arduino.

If Statement

In this statement, we have an expression placed in parenthesis, followed by a statement or a block of statements. If the expression evaluates to True, then the statement (s) will be executed, otherwise, it/they will be skipped.

It takes the following syntax:

if (expression)
   statement;
or the following:
if (expression) {
   Block of statements;
}

Consider the following example:

/* Declaration of a global variable */
int X = 4 ;
int Y = 8 ;

Void setup () {

}

Void loop () {
   /* checking our boolean condition */
   if (X > Y) /* if the condition is true,execute the following statement*/

   X++;

```
/* checking the boolean condition */
  If ( ( X < Y ) && ( Y != 0 )) /* if the condition is true,
execute the following statement*/ {

    X += Y;
    Y--;
  }
}
```

If...else Statement

This has an additional "else" statement which will be executed
if the expression evaluates to a false. It takes the following
syntax:

```
if (expression) {
  statement(s);
}
else {
  statement(s);
}
```

Consider the following example:

```
/* Declaration of a global variable */
int X = 4 ;
int Y = 8 ;

Void setup () {

}

Void loop () {
  /* checking the boolean condition */
  if (X > Y) /* if condition evaluates to true, execute
the following statement*/ {

    X++;
  }else {
```

```
        Y -= X;
    }
}
```

If...else if..else Statement

With this statement, one can test several conditions. It takes the syntax given below:

```
if (expression_1) {
   statement(s);
}

else if(expression_2) {
   statement(s);
}
.
.
.

else {
   statement(s);
}
```

Consider the example given below:

```
/* Global variable definition */
int X = 4 ;
int Y = 8 ;
int z = 14;

Void setup () {

}

Void loop () {
   /* checking the boolean condition */
   if (X > Y) /* if the condition is true, execute the
following statement*/ {

      X++;
   }
   /* checking the boolean condition */
```

```
   else if ((X == Y )||( Y < z) ) /* if the condition is true,
     execute the following statement*/ {
     Z = Y* X;
   }else
     z++;
}
```

Switch case statement

In this case, the programmer has to set a number of cases which will be executed in case certain conditions are fulfilled. It works by comparing the values which have been specified in a variable to the ones which are specified in a case. If a case statement matching the variable which has been specified in the variable is met, the code for the case is then executed.

The switch statement will not exit if we fail to use the "break" keyword, so ensure that you include this.

The following is the syntax for a switch case statement:

```
switch (variable) {
  case label:
  // statement(s)
  break;
}

case label: {
  // statement(s)
  break;
}

default: {
  // statement(s)
  break;
}
```

Consider the example given below:

```
switch (phase) {
  case 0: Enter(); break;
  case 1: Good(); break;
  case 2: Two(); break;
  default: Message("Invalid value!");
}
```

Conditional Operator

This is represented as "?:" and it forms the only ternary operator in this language. It takes the syntax given below:

expression1 ? expression2 : expression3

The compiler evaluates "expression1.. If its value is found to be true, the "expression2" will be evaluated, and then the "expression3" will be ignored. If the "expressions1" is found to be false, then "expression3" will be evaluated, but "expression2" will be ignored. The result in this case will be the value of the expression2 or expression3 based on the one which evaluates to True.

This operator has a right to left associate.

Consider the example given below:

```
/* Find max(x, y): */
max = ( x > y ) ? x : y;
/* Convert a small letter to a capital: */
/* (no parentheses will actually be necessary) */
z = ( z >= 'x' && z <= 'c' ) ? ( z - 32 ) : z;
```

The following are rules for the conditional operator:

1. The expression1 has to be a scalar operation. The expression2 and expression3 have to obey one of the rules given below.

2. The two expressions have to be passed through the normal arithmetic conversions and this will determine the type which results.

3. The expressions have to take a void type. The type which results should be void.

Chapter 7- Loops in Arduino

With loops, we are able to execute a statement or a block of statements in a number of multiple times. Let us discuss the loops which are supported in Arduino.

The "while" loop

The execution of the while loop continues until the expression placed inside parenthesis () is found to be false. If the variable under test is not changed, then the loop will exit.

It takes the following syntax:

```
while(expression) {
   Statement(s);
}
```
Consider the following example:

```
var = 0;
while(var < 50){
  // perform an action repetitively for 50 times
  var++;
}
```

The "do...while" Loop

This works in a similar way to the "while" loop. In the "while" loop, the test condition is created before the body of the loop. In the "do...while" loop, the test condition is placed after the body of the loop.

After termination of the "do...while," the execution process will continue to the clause after your "while" clause. It takes the following syntax:

```
do {
   statement(s);
}
```

while (expression);
Consider the example given below:

```
do
{
  delay(40);          // wait for the sensors to become stable

  x = readSensors();  // check your sensors

} while (x < 90);
```

The "for" Loop

This loop will execute for a specified number of times. The expression for controlling the execution has to be initialized, tested, and then manipulated in the parenthesis for the loop.

The loop must have a maximum of three expressions which are responsible for determination of execution. It takes the following syntax:

```
for ( initialize; control; increment or decrement) {
  // statement(s)
}
```

Consider the example given below:

```
for(counter = 0;counter <= 5;counter++) {
  //statement(s) to be executed
}
```

Nested Loop

In Arduino, it is possible for us to use a loop inside another loop. This is done following the syntax given below:

```
for ( initialize ;control; increment or decrement) {
  // statement(s)
```

```
for ( initialize ;control; increment or decrement) {
   // statement (s)
   }
}
```

Consider the example given below:

```
for(counter = 0;counter <= 8;counter++) {
   //statement(s) to be executed
   for(j = 0;j <= 99;j++) {
      //statement(s) to be executed
   }
}
```

Infinite Loop

This is a kind of a loop which has no termination condition, which will make it to execute infinitely.

This can be created as follows:
The "for" Loop

This one takes the following syntax:

```
for (;;) {
   // statement (s)
}
```

The "while" Loop

This should be implemented with the following syntax:

```
while(1) {
   // statement (s)
}
```

The "do...while" Loop

This should be implemented with the syntax given below:

```
do {
  statement(s);
}
while(1);
```

Chapter 8- Functions

Functions allow us to group our code into sections so as to perform different tasks. If you need to perform a similar task for a number of times in a program, then the best mechanism is for you to create a function. This is good for helping the programmer to stay organized. The code used in a program is also made smaller and a bit compact.

An Arduino program or sketch requires two functions, that is, sketch () and loop (). We discussed these earlier in this book. For you to create other functions, then you have to do it outside the brackets for these functions. Function definition takes the following as the common syntax:

Return_type function_name (argument1, argument2)
{
      Statements
}

Function Declaration

A function has to be declared outside the other functions. Declaration of functions can be done in two different methods: In the first method, one has to write the part of a method named "function prototype" above the loop function, and this should have the following parts:

- Return type for the function

- Function name

- Argument type for the function

Note that the function prototype has to be followed by a semicolon (;). This is best demonstrated in the example given below:

```
int sum_func (int a, int b)
// function declaration {
   int c = 0;
   c = a+b ;
   return c; // return the value
}

void setup () {
   Statements // the group of statements
}

Void loop () {
   int result = 0 ;
   result = Sum_func (4,8) ; // function call
}
```

In the second part, which involves the function declaration, you have to do it below the loop function. This is made up of the following parts:

- Return type for the function

- Function name

- Function argument type

- Function body

This can be done as shown in the example given below:

```
int sum_func (int , int ) ; // the function prototype
void setup () {
  Statements // the group of statements
}

Void loop () {
  int result = 0 ;
  result = Sum_func (4,8) ; // the function call
}

int sum_func (int a, int b) // the function declaration
{

  int c = 0;
  c = a+b ;
  return c; // return the value
}
```

Chapter 9- Inter Integrated Circuit

This is a circuit for exchanging serial data between the microcontrollers and special integrated circuits. This is used when there is a short distance between these two. The connection has to be established between two conductors. One of them is used for data synchronization, while the other is used for data transfer.

Board I2C Pins

The 12C bus is made up of two signals, the SLC and the SDA. SLC refers to the clock signal, while the SDA is the data signal. The bus master is responsible for the generation of the clock signal.

Arduino boards have the following different pins:

- Uno, Pro Mini A4 (SDA), A5 (SCL)

- Leonardo, Yun 2 (SDA), 3 (SCL)

- Mega, Due 20 (SDA), 21 (SCL)

Arduino I2C

There are two modes, that is, slave code and master code, for connection of two Arduino boards by use of 12C. These include the following:

- Master Transmitter / Slave Receiver

- Master Receiver / Slave Transmitter

Master Transmitter

The functions given below can be used for initialization of the wire library and then join the 12C bus as the master slave:

1. Wire.begin(address)- the address is the slave address in a 7-bit format.

2. Wire.beginTransmission(address)- this launches the transmission to 12C slave device with a given address.

3. Wire.write(value)- this is for queuing bytes for transmission from the master to the slave device.

4. Wire.endTransmission()- this will terminate the transmission to the slave device which was started by the beginTransmission(), and the bytes queued by the wire.write() will be transmitted.

Consider the following example:

```
#include <Wire.h>
//including the wire library
void setup()
//this is to be executed only once
{
  Wire.begin();
//will join the i2c bus as a master
}

short age = 0;

void loop() {
  Wire.beginTransmission(2);
```

```
// transmit to the device #2
Wire.write("The age is = ");
Wire.write(age);
// only one byte will be sent
Wire.endTransmission();
// stopping the transmission
delay(1000);
}
```

Slave Receiver

We use the following functions:

1. Wire.begin(address)- the address refers to the 7-bit slave address.

2. Wire.onReceive(received data handler)- this is the function which will be called once the slave device has received data from the master.

3. Wire.available()- this will return the number of bytes available to be retrieved with the "Wire.read()." This has to be called inside the handler named "Wire.onReceive()."

Consider the following example:

```
#include <Wire.h>
//include the wire library
void setup() {
//this will be executed for only once
Wire.begin(2);
// join the i2c bus with the address #2
Wire.onReceive(receiveEvent);
Serial.begin(9600);
```

```
// start the serial for the output to print the received
content

}

void loop() {
  delay(250);
}

//-----the function will be run once data has been
received from the master-----//

void receiveEvent(int howMany) {
  while (Wire.available()>1)
last {
    char c = Wire.read();
// receive the byte like a character
    Serial.print(c);
// printing the character
  }
}
```
Master Receiver

The master is configured so that it can make a request, and
read some bytes of data sent from Slave Arduino with a unique
address.

Consider the following example:

```
#include <Wire.h> /
/including wire library
void setup() {
  Wire.begin();
// join the i2c bus
  Serial.begin(9600);
```

35

```
// Launch the serial for output
}

void loop() {
  Wire.requestFrom(2, 1);
// request a byte from the slave device #2
  while (Wire.available())
// the slave can send less than what is requested
  {
    char c = Wire.read();
// receive the byte as a character
    Serial.print(c);
// print the character
  }
  delay(500);
}
```

Slave Transmitter

The function "Wire.onRequest(handler)" is called if the master requests data from the slave device. Consider the following example:

```
#include <Wire.h>
void setup() {
  Wire.begin(2);
// join the i2c bus with an address #2
  Wire.onRequest(requestEvent);
// registering an event
}

Byte x = 0;

void loop() {
  delay(100);
}
```

```
// function to be executed once data has been
requested //by the master

// the function is registered as if it is an event,
consider //setup()

void requestEvent() {
  Wire.write(x);
// responding with a message of a byte as the master
//expects

  x++;
}
```

Chapter 10- I/O Functions

The Arduino board pins can be configured either as inputs or as outputs. The Arduino analog pins can be configured and then used just as the digital pins.

Pin Mode() Function

This function is used for configuration of a specific pin so as to act either as an input or output. The INPUT_PULLUP mode can be used for enabling our internal pull-up resistors. The INPUT mode is then use for disabling the internal pull-ups. This function takes the following syntax:

Void setup () {
  pinMode (pin , mode);
}

The following are the parameters used:

1. pin- this is the pin number which is to be set.

2. mode- this can be in the INPUT, OUTPUT, or the INPUT_PULLUP.

Consider the example given below:

int button = 5 ;
// button has been connected to pin 5
int LED = 6;
// LED has been connected to pin 6

void setup () {

```
  pinMode(button , INPUT_PULLUP);
  // setting the digital pin as the input with the pull-up
//resistor

  pinMode(button , OUTPUT);
// setting a digital pin as the output
}

void setup () {
  If (digitalRead(button ) == LOW)
 // if the button is pressed
{
    digitalWrite(LED,HIGH);
// turn the led on
    delay(500);
// delay it for 500 ms
    digitalWrite(LED,LOW);
// turn the led off
    delay(500);
// delay it for 500 ms
  }
}
```

digitalWrite() Function

This function is used for the writing of a LOW or HIGH value to the digital pin. If the configuration of the pin is set to OUTPUT with the pinMode() function, the voltage will have to be set to the corresponding value, that is, 0V for LOW and 5V for HIGH. If the configuration of the pin is set as INPUT, the digitalWrite() function will disable the LOW or enable the HIGH internal pull up on your input pin.

The "digitalWrite()" function takes the following syntax:

```
Void loop() {
  digitalWrite (pin ,value);
}
```

The following is a description of the parameters used in the above function:

1. pin- this is the pin number which is to be set.
2. mode- this can be in the HIGH or LOW.

Consider the example given below:

```
int LED = 6;
// LED has been connected to the pin 6
void setup () {
  pinMode(LED, OUTPUT);
// the digital pin has been set as the output
}

void setup () {
  digitalWrite(LED,HIGH);
// turn the led on
```

```
  delay(500);
// delay for 500 ms
  digitalWrite(LED,LOW);
// turn the led off
  delay(500);
// delay for 500 ms
}
```

The "analogRead( )" function

Arduino usually detects whenever voltage has been connected to any of its pins, and this is reported through the "analogRead()" function. A difference exists between an analog sensor and the on/off sensor. The former sensor is changing, and this is why a different pin is needed for us to be able to read that sensor.

The function takes the following syntax:

analogRead(pin);

Consider the example given below:

```
int analogPin = 3;
//potentiometer wiper
  // connected to the analog pin 3
int val = 0;
// variable for storing the value which has been read

void setup() {
  Serial.begin(9600);
 // setup serial
}

void loop() {
```

```
  val = analogRead(analogPin);
// reading our input pin
  Serial.println(val);
// the debug value
}
```

Chapter 11- Sample Arduino Projects

Wireless Communication

Both the wireless receiver and transmitter function at 315 Mhz. They can easily fit into a breadboard and be linked nicely with microcontrollers for the creation of a simple wireless data link.

The following are the specifications for the receiver module:

- Product Model – MX-05V

- Quiescent Current – 4mA

- Size – 30 * 14 * 7mm

- Receiving frequency – 315Mhz

- Operating voltage – DC5V

- Receiver sensitivity – -105DB

The following are the specifications for the transmitter module:

- Product Model – MX-FS-03V

- An external antenna, 25cm for single-core line or ordinary multi-core

- Operating voltage, range, 3.5-12V

- Dimensions, 19 * 19mm

- Transmitting power – 10mW

- Operating mode – AM

- Transfer rate – 4KB / S

- Launch distance , range, 20-200 meters

- Transmitting frequency – 315Mhz

- Pinout from left → right, (DATA; V_{CC}; GND)

You should have the following with you:

- 2 × Arduino UNO board

- 1 × Rf link receiver

- 1 × Rf link transmitter

Steps

Begin by connecting your equipment together.

Once done, launch the Arduino IDE from your computer. Click on "New" so as to create a new sketch file.

Note that the keyboard library has to be included in the Arduino library file. Copy the file "VirtualWire.lib," and then paste it in your folder for libraries.

The following should be the code for the transmitter:

```
#include <VirtualWire.h>
char *controller;

void setup() {
  pinMode(13,OUTPUT);
  vw_set_ptt_inverted(true);
  vw_set_tx_pin(12);
  vw_setup(4000);
// data transfer speed in Kbps
}

void loop() {
  controller="1" ;
  vw_send((uint8_t *)controller, strlen(controller));
  vw_wait_tx();
// Wait for the whole message to go
  digitalWrite(13,1);
  delay(2000);
  controller="0" ;
  vw_send((uint8_t *)controller, strlen(controller));
```

```
  vw_wait_tx();
// Wait for the whole message to go
  digitalWrite(13,0);
  delay(2000);
}
```

The code is very simple. First, it will send "1" and then "0" after a few seconds.

The receiver code should be as follows:

```
#include <VirtualWire.h>

void setup() {
  vw_set_ptt_inverted(true);
// Needed for the DR3100
  vw_set_rx_pin(12);
  vw_setup(4000);
// Bits per sec
  pinMode(5, OUTPUT);
  vw_rx_start();
}

void loop() {
  uint8_t buf[VW_MAX_MESSAGE_LEN];
  uint8_t buflen = VW_MAX_MESSAGE_LEN;
  if (vw_get_message(buf, &buflen))
// Non-blocking
{
    if(buf[0]=='1') {
      digitalWrite(5,1);
    }
    if(buf[0]=='0') {
      digitalWrite(5,0);
    }
  }
```

}

The LED which has been connected to the pin 5 on the board has been turned ON.

Blinking LED

LEDs are lights, small and powerful, but used in a wide variety of applications. We need to demonstrate how we can blink the LEDs.

Ensure that you have the following tools with you:

- 1 × 330Ω Resistor

- 1 × Breadboard

- 1 × LED

- 2 × Jumper

- 1 × Arduino Uno R3

Steps

Set up your components on the breadboard. The following diagram can help you in this.

You have to closely look at the LEDs so as to know its poles. The shorter one is the negative terminal.

Launch the Arduino IDE on the computer. Click on "New" so as to open a new sketch.

Add the following Arduino code:

```
/*
 Blink
 Will turns the LED on for a second, then off for a
 second, repeatedly.

*/

// the setup function will execute once once you have
pressed the power or the reset on the board

void setup() {
// initializing the digital pin number 13 as the output.
  pinMode(2, OUTPUT);
```

```
}

// the loop function will run repetitively infinitely

void loop() {
  digitalWrite(2, HIGH);
// turning the LED on
  delay(1000);
// wait for 1 second
  digitalWrite(2, LOW);
// turning the LED off by reducing the voltage to LOW
  delay(1000);
// wait for 1 second
}
```

At this point, you should observe the LED begin to turn on and then off. If you fail to see this, then you have to correctly reconnect the circuit. You can then upload your code to the board and then observe what will happen.

How to Read the Analog Voltage

The analog pin 0 can be read for the analog voltage. This is done by converting the analogRead() to voltage. This will then be printed to our serial monitor of our IDE.

Assemble the following components:

- 1 × 5K variable resistor

- 1 × Breadboard

- 2 × Jumper

- 1 × Arduino Uno R3

Steps

Begin by connecting your components on the breadboard.

Launch your Arduino IDE on the computer, and then create a new sketch file.

Add the following Arduino code to the file:

```
/*
  ReadAnalogVoltage
  Will read the analog input on the pin 0, and then
convert it into voltage, and then print the result to
serial monitor.

  Graphical representation is present by use of serial
plotter (Tools > Serial Plotter menu)

  The central pin of a potentiometer should be
attached to pin A0, while the outside pins should be
attached to +5V and ground.

*/

// the setup routine will execute once  you press
//reset:

void setup() {
  // initializing the serial communication at speed of
//9600 bits per second:

  Serial.begin(9600);
}
```

```
// the loop routine will execute  over and over again
//infinitely:

void loop() {
  // reading the input on the analog pin 0:
  int sensorValue = analogRead(A0);
  // Converting the analog to a voltage
  float voltage = sensorValue * (5.0 / 1023.0);
  // print out the read value:
  Serial.println(voltage);
}
```

You will then be done. You will see a stream of numbers which range between 0.0 and 0.5. Once you turn the pot, you will see the values begin to change.

Keyboard Message in Arduino

We want to create a project in which after a button has been pressed, the string will have to be sent to the computer as the keyboard input. You just have to program the Leonardo and then wire it up. The results will be seen once you have opened the text editor.

Note that after the use of the command "Keyboard.print()," Arduino will take over control of the keyboard of your computer. However, you may not need to lose the control of the keyboard during the sketching process. This can be achieved by setting up a reliable control system before you can call the Keyboard.print() command.

Assemble the following components:

- 1 × Breadboard

- 1 × momentary pushbutton

- 1 × Arduino Micro, Leonardo, or Due board

- 1 × 10k ohm resistor

Steps

Connect you components together, and hook them on the breadboard.

Launch the Arduino IDE on the computer. Click on "New" so as to create a new sketch file. Add the following Arduino code to the file:

```
/*
  Keyboard Message test in Micro and Arduino Leonardo

  Will send a text string once a button has been pressed.

  The circuit:
  * pushbutton has been attached from the pin 4 - +5V
  * 10-kilohm resistor has been attached to pin 4 – ground

*/

#include "Keyboard.h"
const int buttonPin = 4;
//the input pin for the pushbutton
int prevButtonState = HIGH;
```

```
// to check for the state of the pushButton
int counter = 0;
// the button push counter

void setup() {
  pinMode(buttonPin, INPUT);
 // create the pushButton pin as an input:
  Keyboard.begin();
// initializing the control over our keyboard:
}

void loop() {
  int buttonState = digitalRead(buttonPin);
// read the pushbutton:
  if ((buttonState != prevButtonState)&& (buttonState == HIGH))

// it has been pressed:
{
    // incrementing the counter for the button
    counter++;
    // typing out the message
    Keyboard.print("The button has been pressed");
    Keyboard.print(counter);
    Keyboard.println(" times.");
  }
  // save the button status as at the current for comparison during next time:
  prevButtonState = buttonState;
}
```

One of the terminals of the pushbutton should be attached to pin 4 of the Arduino. The other one has to be attached to the 5V. The resistor should be used as the pull-down so as to provide the reference to ground. This means that it has to be attached from pin 4 to ground.

After programming the board, unplug your USB cable, open the text editor, and then move the cursor to the typing area. The keyboard should then be connected to the computer via the USB, and then the button pressed for writing.

Fading LED

We can also use the function "analogWrite()" so as to fade some LED off. The function makes use of pulse width modulation so as to quickly turn the LED on and off so as to create this fading effect.

Assemble the components listed below:

- 1 × 330Ω Resistor

- 1 × Breadboard

- 1 × LED

- 1 × Arduino Uno R3

- 2 × Jumper

Steps

Connect all the above components on the breadboard. Ensure that the terminals have been bent up to 90 degrees so as to fit properly into the sockets of the breadboard. You may also choose to cut the terminals shorter.

Launch the Arduino IDE on the computer, and then create a new file by clicking on "New."

Add the following Arduino code to it:

```
/*
  Fade effect
  Demonstrating how to fade LED on the pin 9 by use
of the analogWrite() function.

  The function makes use of PWM, meaning that
before you can change a pin, ensure that you are
using another PWM capable pin. In most Arduino,
PWM pins are usually identified with   a "~" sign, like
~3, ~5, ~6, ~9, ~10 and ~11.

*/

int led = 9;
//  PWM pin which LED has been attached to
int brightness = 0;
 // the brightness of the LED
int fadeAmount = 5;
// the points the LED is to be fade by
// the setup routine will run only once once you have
//pressed the reset:

void setup() {
  // declaring pin 9 as the output:
  pinMode(led, OUTPUT);
}

// the loop routine will execute over and over again
//infinitely:

void loop() {
  // setting the brightness of the pin 9:
  analogWrite(led, brightness);
```

```
// adjust the brightness for the incoming time via
the //loop:
  brightness = brightness + fadeAmount;
  // reverse the fade direction after each of the fades:
  if (brightness == 0 || brightness == 255) {
    fadeAmount = -fadeAmount ;
  }
  // delay for a period of 30 milliseconds so as to
observe //the dimming effect

  delay(300);
}
```

Once pin 9 has been declared to be the LED pin, then there will be nothing for you to do in setup () function of the code. Two arguments are required in the analog Write () function used in the loop. One of the arguments is to be used for instructing the function to write to the specified pin, while the other argument will indicate the value of PWM which is to be written.

For the LED to be faded on and off you just have to increase the values of the PWM and these should range from 0 to 255, so that the cycle can be completed. After each loop in our example above, the value of "fadeAmound" will be increased by the variable value.

Chapter 12- Mouse Button Control

With the Mouse Library, we can use the Leonardo, Micro, or Due for Arduino so as to control the movement of the mouse cursor.

In our example, we will be using 5 pushbuttons so as to move the onscreen cursor. One button will be for left mouse click, while the other four buttons will be directional. The movement of the cursor from the Arduino is always relative. After an input has been read, the position of the cursor has to be updated in respect to its current position.

After pressing any of the directional buttons, the mouse will be moved by Arduino, and a HIGH input will be mapped to a range of 5 in the correct direction.

The 5th button is responsible for control of a left click on the mouse. The event is recognized after release of the button.

Begin by assembling the following components:

- 5 × 10k ohm resistor

- 1 × Breadboard

- 5 × momentary pushbuttons

- 1 × Arduino Leonardo, Micro, or Due board

Steps

Begin by connecting the components on the breadboard.

Launch the Arduino IDE on the computer. Click on New so as to create a new text file.

Add the following code to the file:

```
#include "Mouse.h"
// set the pin numbers for five buttons:
const int upButton = 2;
const int downButton = 3;
const int leftButton = 4;
const int rightButton = 5;
const int mouseButton = 6;
int range = 5;
// the output range for X or Y movement; it will affect
the speed of movement

int resDelay = 10;
// the response delay for mouse in ms

void setup() {
  // initialization of the buttons' inputs:
  pinMode(upButton, INPUT);
  pinMode(downButton, INPUT);
  pinMode(leftButton, INPUT);
  pinMode(rightButton, INPUT);
  pinMode(mouseButton, INPUT);
  // initialization of mouse control:
  Mouse.begin();
}

void loop() {
  // reading the buttons:
  int upState = digitalRead(upButton);
  int downState = digitalRead(downButton);
```

```
  int rightState = digitalRead(rightButton);
  int leftState = digitalRead(leftButton);
  int clickState = digitalRead(mouseButton);
  // calculating the movement distance depending on
button states:
  int xDistance = (leftState - rightState) * range;
  int yDistance = (upState - downState) * range;
  // if the X or Y is not zero, move:
  if ((xDistance != 0) || (yDistance != 0)) {
    Mouse.move(xDistance, yDistance, 0);
  }

  // after mouse button has been pressed:
  if (clickState == HIGH) {
    // if the mouse has not been pressed, press it:
    if (!Mouse.isPressed(MOUSE_LEFT)) {
      Mouse.press(MOUSE_LEFT);
    }
  } else {
// otherwise, mouse button will not be pressed:
    // if the mouse has been pressed, release it:
    if (Mouse.isPressed(MOUSE_LEFT)) {
      Mouse.release(MOUSE_LEFT);
    }
  }
  // a delay for preventing the mouse from moving too
fast:
  delay(resDelay);
}
```

Use the micro-USB cable to connect the board to the computer. The buttons should be connected to the digital inputs, that is, pins 2 to 6. The used resistors should be 10k pull-down.

Keyboard Logout

In this example, we will use the keyboard library for logging out a user session on the computer once pin 2 on ARDUINO UNO has been pulled to the ground. The sketch will work by simulating the keypress in a sequence of keys (two to three) and these will be released after a short while.

Begin by assembling the following components:

- 1 × Jumper

- 1 × Breadboard

- 1 × pushbutton

- 1 × Arduino Micro, Leonardo, or Due board

Steps

Begin by assembling the components and hooking them on the breadboard.

Launch the Arduino IDE on the computer. Click on New to create a new text file.

Note that the keyboard library has to be included in the Arduino library file. The following should be the Arduino code for the project:

#include "Keyboard.h"

// this should be changed for your platform to be //matched
int platform = WINDOWS;

void setup() {

```
// change the pin 2 to be an input and then turn on
the
// pullup resistor to go high unless it has been
// connected to ground:

pinMode(2, INPUT_PULLUP);
Keyboard.begin();
}

void loop() {
  while (digitalRead(2) == HIGH) {
    // no actionto be done until the pin 2 has gone low
    delay(500);
  }

  delay(1000);

  switch (platform) {
    case OSX:
    Keyboard.press(KEY_LEFT_GUI);

    Keyboard.press(KEY_LEFT_SHIFT);
    Keyboard.press('Q');
    delay(100);

    // enter key:
    Keyboard.write(KEY_RETURN);
    break;

    case WINDOWS:
    // CTRL-ALT-DEL:
    Keyboard.press(KEY_LEFT_CTRL);
    Keyboard.press(KEY_LEFT_ALT);
    Keyboard.press(KEY_DELETE);
    delay(100);
    Keyboard.releaseAll();

    //ALT-l key:
    delay(2000);
```

```
      Keyboard.press(KEY_LEFT_ALT);
      Keyboard.press('l');
      Keyboard.releaseAll();
      break;

      case UBUNTU:
      // CTRL-ALT-DEL:
      Keyboard.press(KEY_LEFT_CTRL);
      Keyboard.press(KEY_LEFT_ALT);
      Keyboard.press(KEY_DELETE);

      delay(1000);
      Keyboard.releaseAll();

      // Hit Enter to confirm the logout:
      Keyboard.write(KEY_RETURN);
      break;
    }

   // no action:
   while (true);
 }

Keyboard.releaseAll();
  // enter key:
    Keyboard.write(KEY_RETURN);
    break;
    case WINDOWS:

  // CTRL-ALT-DEL:
    Keyboard.press(KEY_LEFT_CTRL);
    Keyboard.press(KEY_LEFT_ALT);
    Keyboard.press(KEY_DELETE);
    delay(100);
    Keyboard.releaseAll();

  //ALT-l:
    delay(2000);
    Keyboard.press(KEY_LEFT_ALT);
```

```
      Keyboard.press('l');
      Keyboard.releaseAll();
      break;

   case UBUNTU:
     // CTRL-ALT-DEL:
     Keyboard.press(KEY_LEFT_CTRL);
     Keyboard.press(KEY_LEFT_ALT);
     Keyboard.press(KEY_DELETE);
     delay(1000);
     Keyboard.releaseAll();

     // Hit Enter to confirm the logout:
     Keyboard.write(KEY_RETURN);
     break;
  }

// no action:
  while (true);
}
```

Before the program can be loaded to the board, ensure that you have set it to the correct OS on the variable for platform.

During the execution of the sketch, the pin 2 will be connected to the ground once you hit the button, and the logout sequence will be sent to the USB which has been connected to the PC.

Note that the connection of pin 2 to the ground leads to a logout operation. The logout is done by use of the following key combination:

- CMD-SHIFT-q On OSX

- CTRL-ALT-DEL, and ENTER on Ubuntu

- CTRL-ALT-DEL and then ALT-l on Windows

LED Bar Graph

We need to create an example for reading analog input at the pin 0 and these values will be converted into voltage. This will then be shown on the serial monitor of the Arduino.

Begin by gathering the following components:

- 2 × Jumper

- 1 × Breadboard

- 1 × 5k ohm variable resistor

- 1 × Arduino Uno R3

- 8 × LED

Steps

Begin by connecting the components on the breadboard.

Launch your Arduino IDE software on the computer and click on New to create a new file. The following should be the Arduino code for this:

```
// the following constants will not change:
const int analogPin = Ao;
// the pin attached to the potentiometer
const int ledCount = 8;
// the LEDs number in our bar graph
int ledPins[] = {2, 3, 4, 5, 6, 7, 8, 9};
// the array of pin numbers for LEDs to be attached to

void setup() {
  // looping over pin array and then set them all to the
//output:

  for (int thLed = 0; thLed < ledCount; thLed++) {
    pinMode(ledPins[thLed], OUTPUT);
  }
}

void loop() {
  // reading our potentiometer:
```

```
int sensReading = analogRead(analogPin);
// mapping our result to the range from 0 to number of //LEDs:

int ledLevel = map(sensReading, 0, 1023, 0, ledCount);

// looping over our LED array:
for (int thLed = 0; thLed < ledCount; thLed++) {
// if the index of the array element is less than ledLevel,

// then turn a pin for the element on:
if (thLed < ledLevel) {
  digitalWrite(ledPins[thLed], HIGH);
}else {
//all the pins higher than our ledLevel will be turned off:

  digitalWrite(ledPins[thLed], LOW);
  }
 }
}
```

You will have to first read the input. The input value will then be mapped to our output range, the ten LEDs in this case. A "for" loop will then be setup for the purpose of iterating over our outputs. If the number of outputs in the series becomes lower than a mapped input range, it will be turned on. Otherwise, it will be turned off.

You will observe the LEDs turn ON one after the other once the value of the analog input has increased and then turnoff one after the other once the reading decreases.

Conclusion

We have come to the end of this book. Arduino is just an open source platform which comes in the form of hardware and software which are easy to use. The hardware is the circuit board which we are able to program and a software program which is the Integrated Development Environment (IDE). The Arduino code is written in the IDE, and it is then uploaded to the board.

Arduino is an easy programming language, meaning that anyone can learn how to program in it. The work even becomes much easier for an individual with some basic knowledge in programming.

You can use Arduino for the creation of applications and in controlling machines in a production environment. For instance, the language is highly used in the training of robots used in production environments. Note that there are different types of Arduino boards, and this is based on the microcontrollers which have been used. Some of the boards come with no programming interface, so you have to buy this one separately.